AF496467

THE BATSFORD COLOUR BOOK OF THE LAKE DISTRICT

THE BATSFORD COLOUR BOOK OF
The Lake District

Text and photographs by
Walt Unsworth

B. T. BATSFORD LTD LONDON

First published 1974

© Walt Unsworth 1974

Filmset by Servis Filmsetting Ltd, Manchester
Printed and bound in Great Britain by William Clowes, Beccles, Suffolk,
for the publishers B. T. Batsford Ltd, 4 Fitzhardinge Street, London W1

ISBN 0 7134 2809 0

Contents

Introduction

During the last 200 years or so no area of Britain has had more praise lavished upon it than the Lake District. What is it about this north-west corner of England that inspires poets and artists and causes visitors to return time and time again to its familiar beauties? The easy answer is the scenery, but this is not the whole of it – after all, there is fine scenery in other parts of the country and if we begin to particularise then the Lake District loses appeal. For example, there is no mountain in the Lake District which has the majesty of form that Tryfan has in Snowdonia, no ridge anything like as savage as those of the Cuillins and no valley as pretty as Dovedale in Derbyshire.

The truth, one suspects, is that in the Lake District the whole is more than a sum of the parts. Each facet of the landscape is not only attractive within itself but it integrates into its surroundings more than its rivals do in other regions. The eye is led on from one glorious feature to the next in a continuous progression until the scene fades into the faraway blue mountains, and you feel compelled to travel towards them, hoping and expecting more delights. And if you do follow the trail you are never disappointed.

And surely this explains the popularity? The Lake District is in direct contrast with life itself, for a trail in life can so often lead to disappointments. In the Lake District every man is a Hassan: a Pilgrim who must always move towards the Last Blue Mountain.

Ever since the time when men ceased to regard mountains with abhorrence the Lake District has attracted those with talent and vision. Some were fortunate enough to be born here: Wordsworth and Romney, for example, or in our own time, Norman Nicholson. Others were offcomers, Southey, De Quincey, Coleridge, Ruskin – these were men of international reputation in the arts. The Lake Poets, and following them, John Ruskin, spread the fame of the Lake District round the world, but the fame would have come in any case during the nineteenth century for when Romanticism was at its height what could be more of a Romantic ideal than the lakes and crags of Lakeland?

Certainly it has some undying charisma that affects every succeeding generation. I find it not insignificant that it was in the Lake District that the National Trust was conceived, the first Youth Hostel in Britain opened, and the first Outward Bound School.

The basic structure of the district is that of a glaciated dome. The central area is comprised of hard lavas and volcanic rocks known as the Borrowdale volcanics – the high central summits such as the Scafells, Gable, Helvellyn and the Langdale Pikes, together with the steep crags, are all of this material. To the north are the more easily eroded shales and slates which give the rounded summits of peaks like Skiddaw, and to the south again there are slates and shales, the Bannisdale series, sometimes overlaid with glacial drift and giving the soft country around Windermere. At the very edge, in the south, limestone appears, giving remarkable crags like those at Whitbarrow.

About ten thousand years ago the glaciers departed and left the bones of the land very much as they are today. Deep glacial valleys were scoured out in a radial pattern and where a moraine dam or some harder rock blocked the valley entrance, lakes were formed. The glaciers also left hanging valleys like Goats Water or Stickle Tarn, and moraine islands like those in Derwentwater. Later on, strong streams brought down material and created alluvial flats like those in Borrowdale or cut lakes into two like Derwentwater and Bassenthwaite or Buttermere and Crummock Water.

In the early days the land was wooded up to about 2,000 feet (like most of England). Neolithic man kept to the tops and his remains can be seen at Castlerigg and elsewhere; the Romans, too, kept to the high ground, for this was frontier country to them and they ran a strategic road over High Street and Hardknott to connect the port of Ravensglass with Penrith and the great Wall.

It was only with the coming of the Norse invaders of the tenth century that clearing of the forests began, and many places of the district have names derived from the Norse. Thwaite, for example, means a clearing, and fell means a hill. When the great abbeys of Furness and Byland gained control of most of the district the clearing continued apace to make grazing land for their sheep. However, not all the woods were destroyed because charcoal was required for the iron bloomeries and for the smelting of copper and lead ores in which the district was rich.

By the age of Elizabeth much of the Lakeland landscape looked very much as it does today. There are, of course, some significant exceptions. At the height of the Romantic period when wealthy residents came to the area, there was a good deal of landscaping done with trees and, of course, the ubiquitous rhododendron. Then, too, the railways brought change – the village of Windermere is entirely a railway creation. None of this affected the central core of high fells, though Man's rapacity soon found expression there, too, by the creation of reservoirs like Thirlmere and Haweswater which are now bloated parodies of former natural lakes, the mines and quarries which are now for the most part going back to nature, and the ghastly wholesale planting of conifers in places like Ennerdale, by the Forestry Commission.

Another feature which is noticeable to anyone who walks in the high fells is the abandonment of the intake land on the sides of the valleys. The uppermost of these small plots of land, enclosed by drystone walls, and painstakingly won from the fells many years ago are now reverting back to bracken as farming is concentrated in the valley bottoms. The economics are such that marginal land is no longer worth the farming –

and this is not just a local phenomenon, for the same thing can be seen in many of the Alpine valleys. Sheep roam the tops as they have for centuries, the hardy Herdwick.

Of the towns in the area, Kendal, Cockermouth and Penrith are all peripheral and though undoubtedly part of the district are too remote from the centres of interest to influence the tourist. Of the rest, Keswick, Ambleside and Windermere (with Bowness) are the chief and any of the three make a good centre from which to explore the area – though in the Lake District it should always be borne in mind that no one centre is convenient for everywhere, because the high and inpenetrable central fells brook little in the way of motor roads. To go from north to south is easy because of the main road connecting Windermere with Ambleside and Keswick, but to go from east to west is much more difficult. Either you drive round (and it can be a very long drive indeed) or you cross one of the high passes such as Honister, Hardknott or Wrynose, where the gradients can be 1 in 3. Even then, you may still have some navigating to do to reach your chosen destination. To reach Wasdale from Keswick, for example, requires considerable route-finding ability on the part of a visitor – though well worth the effort.

It is for this reason that the walker has all the advantages in the Lake District. Not only does he see the finest views and feel the excitement of traversing rocky ridges, but walking is often more convenient. By taking a bus to Seatoller, for instance, a good walker can be in Wasdale in a couple of hours from Keswick, having crossed Sty Head.

However, it is not given to all of us to be so active and there are dangers to the unwary in fell-walking. Try it, by all means – but make sure you are well equipped with the right clothes and boots and that you know how to use a map and compass. On a bright summer's day you will catch no harm from a stroll up Skiddaw, but beware uncertain weather. In winter, of course, the high fells are the preserve of the experienced fell-walker and climber (or should be, though not everyone heeds the warnings of the mountain rescue teams). Remember, too, that some of the photographs shown in this book are simply not obtainable by an ordinary camera enthusiast unless he also happens to be an experienced mountaineer!

Not all the walks in the Lake District are long and arduous treks over the fells, of course. There are many simple strolls along the valley paths, or those amiable tracks which climb up the fells but never get serious about it – the old pack horse track from Grange to Seatoller in Borrowdale, for example, or the walk along Loughrigg Terrace with its superb views of Grasmere. Walks such as these abound in the Lake District and every one has some special delight to offer.

The lakes which give the district its name all have their own characteristics so that one is never quite like another. There are 15 of them, if we include little Elterwater. Windermere is the longest – $10\frac{1}{2}$ miles from Lakeside to Waterhead, and Wastwater is the deepest. Each lake varies according to season and, indeed, according to the direction from which it is approached.

And this applies even more so to the fells themselves. Bowfell seen from Scafell looks quite a different fell to the Bowfell one sees from Langdale, or the lumpy contours of the Helvellyn one sees from Thirlspot are hardly reconcilable with the grandeur of the Ullswater side of the mountain. Similarly with the seasons: the green of summer gives way to the flaming gold of autumn as the bracken dies, whilst in winter the fells assume an Alpine quality.

The highest fell of all is Scafell Pike (3,206 feet), which also makes it the highest peak in England. It is separated by a deep gash called Mickledore from Scafell (3,162 feet), the second highest peak and a rather more difficult proposition to climb than its bigger brother. Only two other fells exceed 3,000 feet – Helvellyn (3,113 feet) and Skiddaw (3,054 feet), but there are 108 fells with summits whose heights lies between 2,000 and 3,000 feet, or about double that number if you count individual tops of the same fell, for quite a number of the fells have secondary summits.

An impressive feature of many of the fells is the great rock crags where the climbers find their enjoyment. Rock-climbing is a skilled sport not to be undertaken by the uninitiated, for the penalties of a mistake are obvious, but many of the crags are noble in their own rights and well worth going to look at. Who could fail to be impressed by the stern grandeur of Scafell Crag above Wasdale, or the seeming inaccessibility of Pillar Rock? Easier for the average tourist to visit, but equally grand, are Dow Crag, which looms over Goat's Water, and Pavey Ark which sweeps like a great crescent of rock above Stickle Tarn.

The tarns themselves are often things of great beauty and the variety is quite immense. Some are placid sheets of water – Burnmoor Tarn or Devoke Water, for example – as gentle as a Cheshire mere, whilst others such as Blea Water or Codale Tarn reflect the savagery of the surrounding fells.

Many tarns are in positions virtually inaccessible to anyone who is not a fell-walker but many others are in the valleys, and it is to the valleys that we must return in our examination of the Lake District, for the valleys contain the hamlets and farms that are the living heart of the district and the valleys form the means of access into the fells.

I think it is fair to say that two valleys attract more visitors than all the rest – Langdale and Borrowdale – and this is not because they are necessarily more beautiful than the others but simply because they are more accessible and each has a convenient centre close at hand. In the case of Langdale, the centre is Ambleside and for Borrowdale, Keswick. Each is quite different.

The road up Langdale twists and turns by the side of the River Brathay, through the hamlet of Skelwith Bridge, with its rapids, and on past the delectable lake of Elterwater to the twin villages of Elterwater and Chapel Stile, with their grey stone cottages, slate quarries and wooded knolls. It is not by accident that the villages and woods crowd the valley at this point, for they stand on a hard rock barrier – unproductive land in the old days when every acre that could be cultivated was valuable. Beyond Chapel Stile the valley begins a great bend and thrusting out into the bend are the majestic forms of the Langdale Pikes, perhaps the most recognisable of the Lakeland peaks. Only where the road ends, near the Old Dungeon Ghyll Hotel, does the head of the valley begin to show itself: a magnificent sweep of fells, round from Pike o' Blisco, over Crinkle Crags, Bowfell and Rossett Pike to the Langdale Pikes themselves, though these last are mostly hidden by the tumbled crags rising up the valley sides.

A minor road, steep and very narrow, twists out of the valley by way of Blea Tarn and Wordsworth's Solitary on its way to Little Langdale, but apart from that all further progress towards the valley head can only be made on foot. But the blue mountains beckon and who knows what may lay beyond!

Langdale is an open valley. It shows its treasures willingly, for once you go beyond Chapel Stile, trees are scarce and the open fellside with the numerous grey crags lies revealed. Borrowdale is not like that. Borrowdale is a valley of secrets, few of which can be gleaned from a car, and this is in itself ironical because Borrowdale is more easily negotiable by car than Langdale and escape can be made at its far end over Honister Pass to Buttermere.

Of course, Borrowdale has what Langdale does not have – a great lake – but it also has many more trees and more little side valleys, half hidden from the too casual traveller. The hamlets, too, are more evenly spread along the valley and they are all picturesque: Grange, with its double bridge; Rosthwaite, which is much more than the narrowing of the road it sometimes appears; Seatoller, at the foot of Honister Pass; and Stonethwaite, whose clustered stone cottages make the archetypal Lakeland hamlet. And in the hills above the valley, connected to it by the narrowest of motor roads, sits tiny Watendlath with its lovely tarn.

Borrowdale is the supreme area for the valley walker because there is so much of interest within its compass. The walk from Grange to the top of Castle Crag is almost without compare, or the short walk from Rosthwaite to Watendlath, or easier still, a visit to that Victorian show-piece, the Bowder Stone. The crags, too, are fairly easy to visit, but trees crowd them in and though they are romantic in their setting, few of them have the grandeur of the Langdale crags. Comb Gill is perhaps the best place for those who like to see rock scenery at its wildest.

It would require a much longer book than this to describe in detail all the valleys of the Lake District and in any case the joys of discovery are rare delights in themselves. The pictures in this book give only an indication of the Lake District's treasures and as for the rest – well, perhaps I could end as Harriet Martineau ended the Preface to her own guide to the Lakes, over a century ago:

'If any think that we have painted it too fair, and that we love it fanatically, let them come and see.'

The Plates

STRIDING EDGE, HELVELLYN

Striding Edge is the most celebrated ridge walk in the Lake District and though it has lost much of the terror it had for our nineteenth-century ancestors it is airy enough to provide plenty of excitement for today's fellwalkers. The start is made up the Grisedale track from Patterdale, then by a long sloping path up the flanks of Patterdale Common to the crest of the ridge. The ridge is broad at first but it soon narrows and presents rocky parapets and pinnacles which have to be crossed. Steep slopes then lead to the summit of Helvellyn.

The views are superb, but it is not for the views that Striding Edge is tackled, rather for the difficulties of the route itself. In winter these increase considerably and Striding Edge becomes the preserve of the trained mountaineer, armed with an ice axe and winter clothing.

There are many other ways up this popular fell, all of them easier than Striding Edge.

AMBLESIDE

Ambleside has been called 'the axle at the wheel of beauty' and there is no doubt that it does command a central position for visiting the dales and fells of the Lake District. It became a town in 1650 when it gained its first charter to hold a market, but its main growth has been during the last century, in keeping with the growth of tourism, and solid Victorian architecture is the keynote of the place.

The Bridge House, shown here, is much older. It was probably built in the late seventeenth century as a garden house, but it is complete with oven and chimney and with an outside staircase to the first floor.

National
Trust

WINDERMERE

Largest of all the lakes, with a regular steamer service plying the $10\frac{1}{2}$ miles between the northern extremity of Waterhead and the southern one of Lakeside. Despite its fitful cross-winds the lake is popular with dinghy sailors, not to mention powered craft of all kinds. Sometimes the water seems alive with boats.

The nearness of Ambleside and Bowness, and the fact that one of the main access roads of the district runs along its eastern shore ensures the lively popularity of this lake, but for those who prefer solitude the western shore has much to offer with its quiet bays and woods.

The Langdale Pikes are amongst the most picturesque of the Lakeland fells and look at their best when seen from across the lake.

GRASMERE

Grasmere and Rydal are physically and culturally the heart of the Lake District. It was here that the Lake Poets mostly gathered. Wordsworth, Hartley Coleridge and De Quincey all lived here for a period and especially Wordsworth who made Rydal Mount his final home. Earlier days, when the poet lived at Dove Cottage with his sister Dorothy, are vividly described in the latter's Journals.

Visitors flock to Grasmere in August to see the Rush Bearing ceremony and the Grasmere Sports but in other months it becomes a centre for some of the pleasant, easy walks so often neglected by those who seek only the heights of Helvellyn or Fairfield. Easedale and Far Easedale, Loughrigg and its Terrace, all offer superb views.

The dominant fell of Grasmere is the curious Helm Crag, seen here mantled in the last snows of winter.

DOVE COTTAGE, GRASMERE

The homely cottage where William and Dorothy Wordsworth lived their frugal lives before fame and fortune smiled on the poet. The cottage is open to the public and the interior has been kept as it was in Wordsworth's day.

The Wordsworths occupied Dove Cottage from 1799 to 1808, but it was then taken over by De Quincey who lived in it for the next 26 years and who stuffed it so full of books he could afford to lend them to Coleridge, 500 a time!

Dove Cottage lies out of the village by half a mile, near to the Ambleside road and forms one of a group. Hartley Coleridge lived in the nearby Rose Cottage for a short time.

MIDDLEFELL, LANGDALE

The farm of Middlefell and the Old Dungeon Ghyll Hotel are traditional starting points for walks and climbs around the head of Langdale. Above the buildings are the steep buttresses of Raven Crag, popular with rock climbers, and above them again the peaks of the Langdale Pikes.

The Langdale Pikes, though not particularly high, are amongst the most shapely peaks in the district and are gathered together in an attractive cluster. Harrison Stickle (2,403 feet) is the highest summit of the Pikes and is well seen in the picture. Dungeon Ghyll is a deep ravine cutting into the fell side below Harrison Stickle and is curiously hidden from below: many visitors mistake the popular Mill Ghyll for Dungeon Ghyll.

In a steep scree gully near Pike of Stickle, another of the summits, an ancient stone axe factory has been discovered.

SIDE PIKE, LANGDALE

A narrow and steep motor road connects Little Langdale with Great Langdale, passing the lovely Blea Tarn and the isolated farmhouse which was Wordsworth's 'Solitary'. Above the road, where it descends steeply into Great Langdale, rises Side Pike (1,187 feet), the smallest and least known of the Langdale 'pikes'.

Side Pike is representative of the many smaller Lakeland fells that go virtually unnoticed by visitors, yet which have an attraction of their own. The climb up the Pike is short but fairly stiff and care is needed to avoid the numerous crags. It gives superb views of the better known 'pikes' across the Langdale valley.

TARN HOWS

Tarn Hows lies in the wooded country between Hawkshead and Coniston. It is a large tarn, and its irregular shape with rocky promontories, tiny islands and tree lined shores, make it an irresistible attraction to thousands of visitors every year.

Though the tarn is the centrepiece, the whole of this area is worthy of exploration and surprisingly little known to most visitors. Glen Mary is one such place and so are Yewdale and Tilberthwaite. Tilberthwaite Gill is a magnificent gorge – but access to its innermost secrets is guarded by waterfalls only to be overcome by experienced scramblers.

GREAT GABLE AND STY HEAD

Great Gable (2,949 feet) is one of the most popular peaks in the Lake District. Though there are steep crags on its northern and southern sides, it can be climbed quite easily from Sty Head and dozens of people make the effort every fine day in summer. The views, especially towards the Scafell massif, are impressive. The fell was one of these given by the Fell and Rock Club to the National Trust in 1923 in memory of Club members who died in the 1914–18 war.

The pass over Sty Head connects Wasdale with Borrowdale and passes the lovely Styhead Tarn.

CONISTON WATER

In some ways Coniston Water is the most placid of the large lakes. It is tucked away in the south of the district, away from the main highways, guarded by narrow twisting roads. It is also set well back from the mountains, and so lacks the grandeur that one associates with Ullswater or Derwentwater.

Only at its northern end do the fells show to any extent: seen from Ruskin's old home at Brantwood, the Old Man of Coniston, Wetherlam and their associated fells make a splendidly composed group rising above the village of Coniston. But even here they are set back and do not dominate the lake itself.

Further south, at Oxen House Bay where the photograph was taken, the scenery is more pastoral still and one is conscious of being on one of the quiet fringes of the Lake District.

NAPES NEEDLE, GREAT GABLE

The Wasdale flanks of Great Gable throw down a series of magnificent rock ridges known as the Great Napes. At the foot of one of these ridges stands the Needle, an obelisk of rock some 60 feet high.

The first ascent of the Needle by Haskett Smith in 1886 is often taken as the birth of rock-climbing as a separate sport, free from the overtones of alpinism from which all mountaineering is descended. It is still popular today and though not a hard climb by modern standards, wear and tear on the small holds makes it distinctly harder every year.

An exciting track runs below the Napes Ridges. Called the Gable Traverse it gives superb views of the ridges and climbers in action, though the best viewpoints, like that of the Dress Circle shown here, can only be reached by determined scrambling.

BORROWDALE

The long valley running south from Keswick is regarded by many visitors as the finest in all Lakeland. Certainly no other can provide the same variety of intimate scenery: crags peeping out of wooded slopes, ancient cottages tucked away into folds of fellside, and becks splashing down over tumbled boulders. It is the epitome of Lakeland.

At the head of the valley lies Seathwaite, a hamlet with the unfortunate reputation of having the highest rainfall in England. Here are the Borrowdale Yews and near them the remains of the famous plumbago mines which provided the black lead for Keswick's pencil industry.

The picture was taken looking down the valley from the Sty Head track.

ROCK CLIMBING

Until the end of the last war, rock climbing was a sport enjoyed by only a few hardy souls, but over the last 30 years with the influence of Outward Bound type courses and the improvements in climbing equipment, it has become one of the boom sports. It is difficult to journey into the fells, especially around Wasdale Head, Borrowdale and Langdale, without meeting climbers festooned with ropes and rucksacks.

As a sport, rock climbing began in the Lake District and the area is still one of the most popular with climbers. There are routes of all standards from easy *Moderates* for novices, to hair raising *Extremely Severes* for experts. Proper equipment and, equally important, proper instruction are necessary before tackling steep rocks like the climb shown here on the Great Napes.

SKIDDAW

Evening light lends charm to the gentle outlines of Lakeland's fourth highest fell. Skiddaw, despite its height and bulk, is the most benign of mountains – 'smiling over the country like a generous gentle lord' as the artist Pennant put it.

It dominates Keswick in a singular fashion because the town lies at the very foot of the mountain and Skiddaw itself is isolated from the other fells round about. It is climbed direct from the town; a popular and easy excursion that in more gracious days was done on ponies, and from the summit wide views open out of Borrowdale and the central fells on the one hand, with the desolate rolling hills known as 'back o' Skidda' ' on the other.

BOWFELL FROM SCAFELL PIKE

Scafell Pike (3,210 feet) is the highest summit in England. It is a bleak summit surmounted by an enormous cairn put there by the thousands of visitors who have made the long ascent from Langdale or Borrowdale. The view is all embracing: here is Wordsworth's description of a fine day in October:

'The vales which we had seen from Esk Hause lay yet in view, and, side by side with Eskdale, we now saw the sister Vale of Donnerdale terminated by the Duddon Sands. But the majesty of the mountains below, and close to us, is not to be conceived. We now beheld the whole mass of Great Gable from its base – the Den of Wastdale at our feet – a gulf immeasurable; Grasmire, and the other mountains of Crummock; Ennerdale and its mountains; and the sea beyond!'

The view across the upper Esk is perhaps the wildest of all, towards Bowfell and Crinkle Crags.

BLENCATHRA

Blencathra is a near neighbour of the more famous Skiddaw, but a very different mountain. Although its northern slopes are gentle it frowns over Threlkeld with a superb south face of distinct ridges and darkened corries which in winter hold the snow well and make superb winter expeditions for the experienced mountaineer.

Scales Tarn occupies the best known of the corries; so deeply set that in olden days people believed the stars were reflected in its surface even at midday. The tarn is flanked on one side by Sharp Edge; a well-named ridge that rivals Striding Edge in airy situations.

Seen from a distance, Blencathra assumes that distinctive shape which has given rise to its other name, Saddleback.

BUTTERMERE

The steep roads descending from Newlands House and Honister Pass meet at the little hamlet of Buttermere which stands on the alluvial flats between the lake of the same name and Crummock Water. The Fish Inn, now much restored, was once the home of Mary, the celebrated Beauty of Buttermere who fell for the charms of John Hatfield, a rogue and bigamist. Hatfield ended on the gallows, but Mary married again and lived to a grand old age. Her story appealed to the Romantic movement and was told by the Lake Poets.

The view towards Honister from the western end of the lake is one of the most idyllic in the district. Fleetwith Pike, with Honister Crag on its left, form the centrepiece of the view and the crag-filled hollow of Warnscale Bottom completes the scene.

GREAT END FROM GRAINS GILL

At Stockley Bridge the path to the head of Borrowdale diverges, one branch going up the popular Sty Head route and the other up the less well known Grains Gill below the flanks of Glaramara. The steep fell sides soon begin to close in as path and beck struggle for possession of the gill. At the top, the grim crags of Great End burst into view.

Great End (2,984 feet) is the most northerly summit of the Scafell group and is usually climbed from Esk Hause *en route* for Scafell Pike. In winter the huge gullies which slash into the crag provide some of the finest ice climbs in the Lake District.

The walk up Grains Gill, past Sprinkling Tarn, and the return by Sty Head to Stockley Bridge is a delightful excursion into the very heart of Lakeland.

CRUMMOCK WATER

The 'other lake' of the Buttermere valley and far larger than Buttermere itself, if not so often mentioned. The view shows the lake from Lanthwaite Green with Hause Point jutting out in the middle distance and beyond that the fells of Red Pike and High Stile.

Scale Beck runs down from the slopes of Red Pike into the lake and on its journey cascades over the highest waterfall in the Lake District. Scale Force, as it is called, was a constant source of admiration to the Victorians who visited it in style by crossing the lake in a boat. Nowadays it is more usual to walk from Buttermere!

GRANGE IN BORROWDALE

Grange stands at the heart of the valley; a cluster of grey stone houses huddling round the end of a famous double-arched bridge. The old road runs from here to Keswick, on the western side of the lake, by Manesty and Brandelhow, offering superb views across Derwentwater of the crags and woods on the far shore.

Above Grange the valley narrows to the Jaws of Borrowdale where Castle Crag stands like a sentinel and the rocks of the eastern flank press in on the river.

The village gained its name because it was once a grange of Furness Abbey.

ASHNESS BRIDGE, DERWENTWATER

The road from Barrow Bay to Watendlath climbs steeply out of the main valley to the old packhorse bridge at Ashness and, just for a short space, gives a remarkable view of Derwentwater with the fells beyond.

Derwentwater contains a number of attractive islands, well wooded, on one of which, Lord's Island, lived the Radcliffes, Earls of Derwentwater. The Radcliffes built up a fortune through their mining interests in the area, but it is their staunch support of the monarchy for which they were best known: one of them died with Richard III on Bosworth field, and the last Earl died on the scaffold after the abortive rising of the Pretender in 1715.

An island of a different sort is the so called Floating Island which appears from time to time. It is a rotting mass of vegetation from the bed of the lake brought to the surface by the trapped gases of decomposition. It floats for a while and then disappears again, whence it came.

Of all the view of Lakeland, Derwentwater from Ashness Bridge is perhaps the one best remembered by generations of visitors.

VALE OF NEWLANDS

From Portinscales a narrow road threads through the woods on the western shore of Derwentwater towards the old inn at Swinside and then twists its way through more open country to the hamlet of Stair. At Stair the Newlands Beck divides the road: one branch climbs the steep pass to Newlands Hause and Buttermere, the other wanders up the valley to Little Town before turning back on itself. Both give superb views of the secluded Vale of Newlands.

It is difficult to imagine this quiet valley as an important mining centre, yet in the days of the first Elizabeth the Goldscope Mine gave both lead and copper, with some gold and silver too, and was one of the richest mines in the Kingdom. There were other mines, too, and their remains can still be seen by those with a quick eye for detail.

But tranquility is the keynote of Newlands today, especially in the fading light of a summer's evening when the crescent moon has already risen.

THE OLD GRAMMAR SCHOOL, HAWKSHEAD

Founded in 1585 by Archbishop Sandys, who was born at the nearby Esthwaite Hall, the Free Grammar School is famous as the place where Wordsworth was educated and where he first felt the stirrings of poetic genius. Not that the budding poet was above the usual schoolboy pranks – he carved his name on his desk, and it can still be seen.

Wordsworth came to the school when he was eight and seems to have enjoyed his years there, despite the strict regimen which dictated that school begin at six in the morning and continue until five at night, during the summer months. He stayed at Ann Tyson's cottage and retained a great affection both for her and his schoolmaster, William Taylor. As De Quincey said, never did a scholar have a more luxurious boyhood.

Hawkshead was a great centre of the woollen industry in bygone days and received a charter in 1608. It is one of the finest preserved villages in Lakeland.

AUTUMN

In the late autumn the Lake District loses the lush green mantel which
has clothed it throughout summer and turns to gold. There is gold of
every hue: deep red coppery gold, the old gold of dying oak leaves, and
bright yellow golds, all mingled in profusion. A little later and the
bracken turns to gold, too, so that the fells and woods alike seem aflame.

The old bridge crosses the Rothay and a road runs from it to Loughrigg Cottage which in 1906 was the holiday home of Woodrow Wilson,
later President of the United States.